THRIVE

ANXÎETY JOURNAL
FOR TEENS

ANXIETY JOURNAL

Name : Taylar Thompson

Phone :

Address :

ANXIETY JOURNAL

⊙ **LOCATION**	Pine Feild	
⚡ **ENERGY**	★★⯪☆☆	
🏃 **ACTIVITY**	★★☆☆☆	
☾ **SLEEP**	★★☆☆☆	

NEGATIVE EVENTS

SYMPTOMS	TRIGGERS
Annoyed	Jeril / Janie

MOOD TRACKER

⬭ N/A (SLEEP)	JOY	NUMBNESS
SADNESS	FEAR	ANGER

NOTES

IM going home
IM excited!

ANXIETY JOURNAL

📍 LOCATION	home	
⚡ ENERGY	☆ ★ ☆ ☆ ☆	
🏃 ACTIVITY	☆ ☆ ★ ☆ ☆	
🌙 SLEEP	☆ ☆ ☆ ★ ☆	

DAILY GOALS

- [ ]
- [ ]
- [ ]

NEGATIVE EVENTS

SYMPTOMS	TRIGGERS

MOOD TRACKER

N/A (SLEEP)	JOY	(NUMBNESS)
(SADNESS)	FEAR	ANGER

NOTES

I regret coming home.

ANXIETY JOURNAL

Location			DAILY GOALS	
⚡ ENERGY	☆ ★ ☆ ☆ ☆		☐	
🏃 ACTIVITY	★ ☆ ☆ ☆ ☆		☐	
🌙 SLEEP	★ ★ ★ ☆ ☆		☐	

NEGATIVE EVENTS

SYMPTOMS	TRIGGERS

MOOD TRACKER

N/A (SLEEP)	JOY	NUMBNESS
SADNESS	FEAR	ANGER

NOTES

ANXIETY JOURNAL

⊙ LOCATION	

		DAILY GOALS
⚡ ENERGY	☆ ☆ ☆ ☆ ☆	☐
🏃 ACTIVITY	☆ ☆ ☆ ☆ ☆	☐
🌙 SLEEP	☆ ☆ ☆ ☆ ☆	☐

NEGATIVE EVENTS

SYMPTOMS	TRIGGERS

MOOD TRACKER

▢ N/A (SLEEP)	▢ JOY	▢ NUMBNESS
▢ SADNESS	▢ FEAR	▢ ANGER

NOTES

ANXIETY JOURNAL

⊙ LOCATION		DAILY GOALS	

⚡ ENERGY	☆ ☆ ☆ ☆ ☆	☐
🏃 ACTIVITY	☆ ☆ ☆ ☆ ☆	☐
🌙 SLEEP	☆ ☆ ☆ ☆ ☆	☐

NEGATIVE EVENTS

SYMPTOMS	TRIGGERS

MOOD TRACKER

	N/A (SLEEP)		JOY		NUMBNESS
	SADNESS		FEAR		ANGER

NOTES

ANXIETY JOURNAL

◎ LOCATION		DAILY GOALS

⚡ ENERGY	☆ ☆ ☆ ☆ ☆
🏃 ACTIVITY	☆ ☆ ☆ ☆ ☆
🌙 SLEEP	☆ ☆ ☆ ☆ ☆

Daily Goals:
- ☐
- ☐
- ☐

NEGATIVE EVENTS

SYMPTOMS	TRIGGERS

MOOD TRACKER

🪣 N/A (SLEEP)	🪣 JOY	🪣 NUMBNESS
🪣 SADNESS	🪣 FEAR	🪣 ANGER

NOTES

ANXIETY JOURNAL

◎ LOCATION	
⚡ ENERGY	☆ ☆ ☆ ☆ ☆
🏃 ACTIVITY	☆ ☆ ☆ ☆ ☆
🌙 SLEEP	☆ ☆ ☆ ☆ ☆

DAILY GOALS

- ☐
- ☐
- ☐

NEGATIVE EVENTS

SYMPTOMS	TRIGGERS

MOOD TRACKER

▢ N/A (SLEEP)	▢ JOY	▢ NUMBNESS
▢ SADNESS	▢ FEAR	▢ ANGER

NOTES	

ANXIETY JOURNAL

◎ LOCATION	
⚡ ENERGY	☆ ☆ ☆ ☆ ☆
🏃 ACTIVITY	☆ ☆ ☆ ☆ ☆
🌙 SLEEP	☆ ☆ ☆ ☆ ☆

DAILY GOALS

- ☐
- ☐
- ☐

NEGATIVE EVENTS

SYMPTOMS	TRIGGERS

MOOD TRACKER

N/A (SLEEP)	JOY	NUMBNESS
SADNESS	FEAR	ANGER

NOTES

ANXIETY JOURNAL

⊙ LOCATION		DAILY GOALS
⚡ ENERGY	☆☆☆☆☆	☐
🏃 ACTIVITY	☆☆☆☆☆	☐
🌙 SLEEP	☆☆☆☆☆	☐

NEGATIVE EVENTS

SYMPTOMS	TRIGGERS

MOOD TRACKER

▽	N/A (SLEEP)	▽	JOY	▽	NUMBNESS
▽	SADNESS	▽	FEAR	▽	ANGER

NOTES	

ANXIETY JOURNAL

◎ LOCATION	
⚡ ENERGY	☆ ☆ ☆ ☆ ☆
🏃 ACTIVITY	☆ ☆ ☆ ☆ ☆
🌙 SLEEP	☆ ☆ ☆ ☆ ☆

DAILY GOALS

- ☐
- ☐
- ☐

NEGATIVE EVENTS

SYMPTOMS	TRIGGERS

MOOD TRACKER

🪣 N/A (SLEEP)	🪣 JOY	🪣 NUMBNESS
🪣 SADNESS	🪣 FEAR	🪣 ANGER

NOTES

ANXIETY JOURNAL

⊙ LOCATION		
⚡ ENERGY	☆ ☆ ☆ ☆ ☆	
🏃 ACTIVITY	☆ ☆ ☆ ☆ ☆	
🌙 SLEEP	☆ ☆ ☆ ☆ ☆	

DAILY GOALS

- ☐
- ☐
- ☐

NEGATIVE EVENTS

SYMPTOMS	TRIGGERS

MOOD TRACKER

▢ N/A (SLEEP)	▢ JOY	▢ NUMBNESS
▢ SADNESS	▢ FEAR	▢ ANGER

NOTES

ANXIETY JOURNAL

LOCATION		DAILY GOALS
⚡ ENERGY	☆ ☆ ☆ ☆ ☆	☐
🏃 ACTIVITY	☆ ☆ ☆ ☆ ☆	☐
🌙 SLEEP	☆ ☆ ☆ ☆ ☆	☐

NEGATIVE EVENTS

SYMPTOMS	TRIGGERS

MOOD TRACKER

N/A (SLEEP)	JOY	NUMBNESS
SADNESS	FEAR	ANGER

NOTES

ANXIETY JOURNAL

◎ **LOCATION**	**DAILY GOALS**
⚡ **ENERGY** ☆☆☆☆☆	☐
🏃 **ACTIVITY** ☆☆☆☆☆	☐
🌙 **SLEEP** ☆☆☆☆☆	☐

NEGATIVE EVENTS

SYMPTOMS	TRIGGERS

MOOD TRACKER

▢ N/A (SLEEP)	▢ JOY	▢ NUMBNESS
▢ SADNESS	▢ FEAR	▢ ANGER

NOTES

ANXIETY JOURNAL

◎ LOCATION		DAILY GOALS

⚡ ENERGY	☆ ☆ ☆ ☆ ☆
🏃 ACTIVITY	☆ ☆ ☆ ☆ ☆
🌙 SLEEP	☆ ☆ ☆ ☆ ☆

DAILY GOALS

- ☐
- ☐
- ☐

NEGATIVE EVENTS

SYMPTOMS	TRIGGERS

MOOD TRACKER

N/A (SLEEP)	JOY	NUMBNESS
SADNESS	FEAR	ANGER

NOTES

ANXIETY JOURNAL

LOCATION	
⚡ ENERGY	☆ ☆ ☆ ☆ ☆
🏃 ACTIVITY	☆ ☆ ☆ ☆ ☆
🌙 SLEEP	☆ ☆ ☆ ☆ ☆

DAILY GOALS

- ☐
- ☐
- ☐

NEGATIVE EVENTS

SYMPTOMS	TRIGGERS

MOOD TRACKER

N/A (SLEEP)	JOY	NUMBNESS
SADNESS	FEAR	ANGER

NOTES

ANXIETY JOURNAL

⊙ LOCATION		
⚡ ENERGY	☆ ☆ ☆ ☆ ☆	
🏃 ACTIVITY	☆ ☆ ☆ ☆ ☆	
🌙 SLEEP	☆ ☆ ☆ ☆ ☆	

DAILY GOALS

- ☐
- ☐
- ☐

NEGATIVE EVENTS

SYMPTOMS	TRIGGERS

MOOD TRACKER

▢ N/A (SLEEP)	▢ JOY	▢ NUMBNESS
▢ SADNESS	▢ FEAR	▢ ANGER

NOTES

ANXIETY JOURNAL

📍 LOCATION		
⚡ ENERGY	☆ ☆ ☆ ☆ ☆	
🏃 ACTIVITY	☆ ☆ ☆ ☆ ☆	
🌙 SLEEP	☆ ☆ ☆ ☆ ☆	

DAILY GOALS

- ☐
- ☐
- ☐

NEGATIVE EVENTS

SYMPTOMS	TRIGGERS

MOOD TRACKER

N/A (SLEEP)	JOY	NUMBNESS
SADNESS	FEAR	ANGER

NOTES

ANXIETY JOURNAL

⊙ LOCATION		DAILY GOALS

⚡ ENERGY	☆ ☆ ☆ ☆ ☆	☐
🏃 ACTIVITY	☆ ☆ ☆ ☆ ☆	☐
🌙 SLEEP	☆ ☆ ☆ ☆ ☆	☐

NEGATIVE EVENTS

SYMPTOMS	TRIGGERS

MOOD TRACKER

⛝ N/A (SLEEP)	⛝ JOY	⛝ NUMBNESS
⛝ SADNESS	⛝ FEAR	⛝ ANGER

NOTES

ANXIETY JOURNAL

LOCATION		DAILY GOALS	
⚡ ENERGY	☆ ☆ ☆ ☆ ☆	☐	
🏃 ACTIVITY	☆ ☆ ☆ ☆ ☆	☐	
🌙 SLEEP	☆ ☆ ☆ ☆ ☆	☐	

NEGATIVE EVENTS

SYMPTOMS	TRIGGERS

MOOD TRACKER

	N/A (SLEEP)		JOY		NUMBNESS
	SADNESS		FEAR		ANGER

NOTES

ANXIETY JOURNAL

◎ LOCATION	
⚡ ENERGY	☆ ☆ ☆ ☆ ☆
🏃 ACTIVITY	☆ ☆ ☆ ☆ ☆
🌙 SLEEP	☆ ☆ ☆ ☆ ☆

DAILY GOALS

- ☐
- ☐
- ☐

NEGATIVE EVENTS

SYMPTOMS	TRIGGERS

MOOD TRACKER

N/A (SLEEP)	JOY	NUMBNESS
SADNESS	FEAR	ANGER

NOTES

ANXIETY JOURNAL

⊙ LOCATION	
⚡ ENERGY ☆ ☆ ☆ ☆ ☆	
🏃 ACTIVITY ☆ ☆ ☆ ☆ ☆	
🌙 SLEEP ☆ ☆ ☆ ☆ ☆	

DAILY GOALS

☐

☐

☐

NEGATIVE EVENTS

SYMPTOMS	TRIGGERS

MOOD TRACKER

N/A (SLEEP)	JOY	NUMBNESS
SADNESS	FEAR	ANGER

NOTES

ANXIETY JOURNAL

⊙ LOCATION	
⚡ ENERGY	☆ ☆ ☆ ☆ ☆
🏃 ACTIVITY	☆ ☆ ☆ ☆ ☆
🌙 SLEEP	☆ ☆ ☆ ☆ ☆

DAILY GOALS

- ☐
- ☐
- ☐

NEGATIVE EVENTS

SYMPTOMS	TRIGGERS

MOOD TRACKER

N/A (SLEEP)	JOY	NUMBNESS
SADNESS	FEAR	ANGER

NOTES

ANXIETY JOURNAL

LOCATION		DAILY GOALS

⚡ ENERGY	☆ ☆ ☆ ☆ ☆
🏃 ACTIVITY	☆ ☆ ☆ ☆ ☆
🌙 SLEEP	☆ ☆ ☆ ☆ ☆

DAILY GOALS

- ☐
- ☐
- ☐

NEGATIVE EVENTS

SYMPTOMS	TRIGGERS

MOOD TRACKER

	N/A (SLEEP)		JOY		NUMBNESS
	SADNESS		FEAR		ANGER

NOTES

ANXIETY JOURNAL

⊙ LOCATION		DAILY GOALS
⚡ ENERGY	☆ ☆ ☆ ☆ ☆	☐
🏃 ACTIVITY	☆ ☆ ☆ ☆ ☆	☐
🌙 SLEEP	☆ ☆ ☆ ☆ ☆	☐

NEGATIVE EVENTS

SYMPTOMS	TRIGGERS

MOOD TRACKER

⬜ N/A (SLEEP)	⬜ JOY	⬜ NUMBNESS
⬜ SADNESS	⬜ FEAR	⬜ ANGER

NOTES	

ANXIETY JOURNAL

⊙ LOCATION	
⚡ ENERGY	☆ ☆ ☆ ☆ ☆
🏃 ACTIVITY	☆ ☆ ☆ ☆ ☆
🌙 SLEEP	☆ ☆ ☆ ☆ ☆

DAILY GOALS

- [ ]
- [ ]
- [ ]

NEGATIVE EVENTS

SYMPTOMS	TRIGGERS

MOOD TRACKER

N/A (SLEEP)	JOY	NUMBNESS
SADNESS	FEAR	ANGER

NOTES

ANXIETY JOURNAL

⊙ LOCATION		DAILY GOALS
⚡ ENERGY	☆ ☆ ☆ ☆ ☆	☐
🏃 ACTIVITY	☆ ☆ ☆ ☆ ☆	☐
🌙 SLEEP	☆ ☆ ☆ ☆ ☆	☐

NEGATIVE EVENTS

SYMPTOMS	TRIGGERS

MOOD TRACKER

▽ N/A (SLEEP)	▽ JOY	▽ NUMBNESS
▽ SADNESS	▽ FEAR	▽ ANGER

NOTES	

ANXIETY JOURNAL

⊙ LOCATION		DAILY GOALS

⚡ ENERGY	☆ ☆ ☆ ☆ ☆	☐
🏃 ACTIVITY	☆ ☆ ☆ ☆ ☆	☐
🌙 SLEEP	☆ ☆ ☆ ☆ ☆	☐

NEGATIVE EVENTS

SYMPTOMS	TRIGGERS

MOOD TRACKER

N/A (SLEEP)	JOY	NUMBNESS
SADNESS	FEAR	ANGER

NOTES

ANXIETY JOURNAL

⊙ LOCATION		DAILY GOALS

⚡ ENERGY	☆ ☆ ☆ ☆ ☆	☐
🏃 ACTIVITY	☆ ☆ ☆ ☆ ☆	☐
🌙 SLEEP	☆ ☆ ☆ ☆ ☆	☐

NEGATIVE EVENTS

SYMPTOMS	TRIGGERS

MOOD TRACKER

	N/A (SLEEP)		JOY		NUMBNESS
	SADNESS		FEAR		ANGER

NOTES

ANXIETY JOURNAL

LOCATION	DAILY GOALS

⚡ ENERGY	☆ ☆ ☆ ☆ ☆	☐
🏃 ACTIVITY	☆ ☆ ☆ ☆ ☆	☐
🌙 SLEEP	☆ ☆ ☆ ☆ ☆	☐

NEGATIVE EVENTS

SYMPTOMS	TRIGGERS

MOOD TRACKER

☐ N/A (SLEEP)	☐ JOY	☐ NUMBNESS
☐ SADNESS	☐ FEAR	☐ ANGER

NOTES

ANXIETY JOURNAL

LOCATION		DAILY GOALS	
⚡ ENERGY	☆☆☆☆☆	☐	
🏃 ACTIVITY	☆☆☆☆☆	☐	
🌙 SLEEP	☆☆☆☆☆	☐	

NEGATIVE EVENTS

SYMPTOMS	TRIGGERS

MOOD TRACKER

	N/A (SLEEP)		JOY		NUMBNESS
	SADNESS		FEAR		ANGER

NOTES

ANXIETY JOURNAL

LOCATION		DAILY GOALS	
⚡ ENERGY	☆ ☆ ☆ ☆ ☆	☐	
🏃 ACTIVITY	☆ ☆ ☆ ☆ ☆	☐	
🌙 SLEEP	☆ ☆ ☆ ☆ ☆	☐	

NEGATIVE EVENTS

SYMPTOMS	TRIGGERS

MOOD TRACKER

	N/A (SLEEP)		JOY		NUMBNESS
	SADNESS		FEAR		ANGER

NOTES	

ANXIETY JOURNAL

◎ LOCATION			DAILY GOALS	
⚡ ENERGY	☆ ☆ ☆ ☆ ☆		☐	
🏃 ACTIVITY	☆ ☆ ☆ ☆ ☆		☐	
🌙 SLEEP	☆ ☆ ☆ ☆ ☆		☐	

NEGATIVE EVENTS

SYMPTOMS	TRIGGERS

MOOD TRACKER

N/A (SLEEP)	JOY	NUMBNESS
SADNESS	FEAR	ANGER

NOTES

ANXIETY JOURNAL

LOCATION		DAILY GOALS	
⚡ ENERGY	☆ ☆ ☆ ☆ ☆	☐	
🏃 ACTIVITY	☆ ☆ ☆ ☆ ☆	☐	
🌙 SLEEP	☆ ☆ ☆ ☆ ☆	☐	

NEGATIVE EVENTS

SYMPTOMS	TRIGGERS

MOOD TRACKER

	N/A (SLEEP)		JOY		NUMBNESS
	SADNESS		FEAR		ANGER

NOTES

ANXIETY JOURNAL

⊙ LOCATION	
⚡ ENERGY	☆☆☆☆☆
🏃 ACTIVITY	☆☆☆☆☆
☾ SLEEP	☆☆☆☆☆

DAILY GOALS

- ☐
- ☐
- ☐

NEGATIVE EVENTS

SYMPTOMS	TRIGGERS

MOOD TRACKER

N/A (SLEEP)	JOY	NUMBNESS
SADNESS	FEAR	ANGER

NOTES

ANXIETY JOURNAL

⊙ LOCATION		DAILY GOALS

⚡ ENERGY	☆ ☆ ☆ ☆ ☆	☐
🏃 ACTIVITY	☆ ☆ ☆ ☆ ☆	☐
🌙 SLEEP	☆ ☆ ☆ ☆ ☆	☐

NEGATIVE EVENTS

SYMPTOMS	TRIGGERS

MOOD TRACKER

	N/A (SLEEP)		JOY		NUMBNESS
	SADNESS		FEAR		ANGER

NOTES	

ANXIETY JOURNAL

⊙ LOCATION	
⚡ ENERGY	☆☆☆☆☆
🏃 ACTIVITY	☆☆☆☆☆
🌙 SLEEP	☆☆☆☆☆

DAILY GOALS

- ☐
- ☐
- ☐

NEGATIVE EVENTS

SYMPTOMS	TRIGGERS

MOOD TRACKER

N/A (SLEEP)	JOY	NUMBNESS
SADNESS	FEAR	ANGER

NOTES

ANXIETY JOURNAL

⊙ LOCATION	
⚡ ENERGY	☆ ☆ ☆ ☆ ☆
🏃 ACTIVITY	☆ ☆ ☆ ☆ ☆
🌙 SLEEP	☆ ☆ ☆ ☆ ☆

DAILY GOALS

- ☐
- ☐
- ☐

NEGATIVE EVENTS

SYMPTOMS	TRIGGERS

MOOD TRACKER

🥛 N/A (SLEEP)	🥛 JOY	🥛 NUMBNESS
🥛 SADNESS	🥛 FEAR	🥛 ANGER

NOTES

ANXIETY JOURNAL

⊙ LOCATION		DAILY GOALS

⚡ ENERGY	☆ ☆ ☆ ☆ ☆
🏃 ACTIVITY	☆ ☆ ☆ ☆ ☆
☾ SLEEP	☆ ☆ ☆ ☆ ☆

DAILY GOALS
- ☐
- ☐
- ☐

NEGATIVE EVENTS

SYMPTOMS	TRIGGERS

MOOD TRACKER

▽ N/A (SLEEP)	▽ JOY	▽ NUMBNESS
▽ SADNESS	▽ FEAR	▽ ANGER

NOTES	

ANXIETY JOURNAL

⊙ LOCATION		DAILY GOALS

⚡ ENERGY	☆ ☆ ☆ ☆ ☆	☐
🏃 ACTIVITY	☆ ☆ ☆ ☆ ☆	☐
🌙 SLEEP	☆ ☆ ☆ ☆ ☆	☐

NEGATIVE EVENTS

SYMPTOMS	TRIGGERS

MOOD TRACKER

N/A (SLEEP)	JOY	NUMBNESS
SADNESS	FEAR	ANGER

NOTES

ANXIETY JOURNAL

◎ LOCATION	
⚡ ENERGY	☆ ☆ ☆ ☆ ☆
🏃 ACTIVITY	☆ ☆ ☆ ☆ ☆
🌙 SLEEP	☆ ☆ ☆ ☆ ☆

DAILY GOALS

- ☐
- ☐
- ☐

NEGATIVE EVENTS

SYMPTOMS	TRIGGERS

MOOD TRACKER

N/A (SLEEP)	JOY	NUMBNESS
SADNESS	FEAR	ANGER

NOTES

ANXIETY JOURNAL

⊙ LOCATION	

⚡ ENERGY	☆ ☆ ☆ ☆ ☆
🏃 ACTIVITY	☆ ☆ ☆ ☆ ☆
🌙 SLEEP	☆ ☆ ☆ ☆ ☆

DAILY GOALS

- ☐
- ☐
- ☐

NEGATIVE EVENTS

SYMPTOMS	TRIGGERS

MOOD TRACKER

🟦	N/A (SLEEP)	🟦	JOY	🟦	NUMBNESS
🟦	SADNESS	🟦	FEAR	🟦	ANGER

NOTES

ANXIETY JOURNAL

⊙ LOCATION	
⚡ ENERGY ☆☆☆☆☆	
🏃 ACTIVITY ☆☆☆☆☆	
☽ SLEEP ☆☆☆☆☆	

DAILY GOALS

☐

☐

☐

NEGATIVE EVENTS

SYMPTOMS	TRIGGERS

MOOD TRACKER

N/A (SLEEP)	JOY	NUMBNESS
SADNESS	FEAR	ANGER

NOTES

ANXIETY JOURNAL

⊙ LOCATION		DAILY GOALS	

⚡ ENERGY	☆ ☆ ☆ ☆ ☆	☐
🏃 ACTIVITY	☆ ☆ ☆ ☆ ☆	☐
🌙 SLEEP	☆ ☆ ☆ ☆ ☆	☐

NEGATIVE EVENTS

SYMPTOMS	TRIGGERS

MOOD TRACKER

⬜ N/A (SLEEP)	⬜ JOY	⬜ NUMBNESS
⬜ SADNESS	⬜ FEAR	⬜ ANGER

NOTES	

ANXIETY JOURNAL

⊙ LOCATION		DAILY GOALS

⚡ ENERGY	☆ ☆ ☆ ☆ ☆	☐
🏃 ACTIVITY	☆ ☆ ☆ ☆ ☆	☐
🌙 SLEEP	☆ ☆ ☆ ☆ ☆	☐

NEGATIVE EVENTS

SYMPTOMS	TRIGGERS

MOOD TRACKER

▢ N/A (SLEEP)	▢ JOY	▢ NUMBNESS
▢ SADNESS	▢ FEAR	▢ ANGER

NOTES	

ANXIETY JOURNAL

⊚ LOCATION		DAILY GOALS	
⚡ ENERGY	☆ ☆ ☆ ☆ ☆	☐	
🏃 ACTIVITY	☆ ☆ ☆ ☆ ☆	☐	
🌙 SLEEP	☆ ☆ ☆ ☆ ☆	☐	

NEGATIVE EVENTS

SYMPTOMS	TRIGGERS

MOOD TRACKER

N/A (SLEEP)	JOY	NUMBNESS
SADNESS	FEAR	ANGER

NOTES	

ANXIETY JOURNAL

◉ LOCATION	
⚡ ENERGY	☆ ☆ ☆ ☆ ☆
🏃 ACTIVITY	☆ ☆ ☆ ☆ ☆
☾ SLEEP	☆ ☆ ☆ ☆ ☆

DAILY GOALS

- ☐
- ☐
- ☐

NEGATIVE EVENTS

SYMPTOMS	TRIGGERS

MOOD TRACKER

▢ N/A (SLEEP)		▢ JOY		▢ NUMBNESS	
▢ SADNESS		▢ FEAR		▢ ANGER	

NOTES

ANXIETY JOURNAL

LOCATION		DAILY GOALS	
⚡ ENERGY	☆☆☆☆☆	☐	
🏃 ACTIVITY	☆☆☆☆☆	☐	
🌙 SLEEP	☆☆☆☆☆	☐	

NEGATIVE EVENTS

SYMPTOMS	TRIGGERS

MOOD TRACKER

▢ N/A (SLEEP)		▢ JOY		▢ NUMBNESS	
▢ SADNESS		▢ FEAR		▢ ANGER	

NOTES	

ANXIETY JOURNAL

⊙ LOCATION	
⚡ ENERGY	☆ ☆ ☆ ☆ ☆
🏃 ACTIVITY	☆ ☆ ☆ ☆ ☆
🌙 SLEEP	☆ ☆ ☆ ☆ ☆

DAILY GOALS

- ☐
- ☐
- ☐

NEGATIVE EVENTS

SYMPTOMS	TRIGGERS

MOOD TRACKER

N/A (SLEEP)	JOY	NUMBNESS
SADNESS	FEAR	ANGER

NOTES

ANXIETY JOURNAL

⊙ LOCATION	
⚡ ENERGY	☆ ☆ ☆ ☆ ☆
🏃 ACTIVITY	☆ ☆ ☆ ☆ ☆
🌙 SLEEP	☆ ☆ ☆ ☆ ☆

DAILY GOALS

- [ ]
- [ ]
- [ ]

NEGATIVE EVENTS

SYMPTOMS	TRIGGERS

MOOD TRACKER

N/A (SLEEP)	JOY	NUMBNESS
SADNESS	FEAR	ANGER

NOTES

ANXIETY JOURNAL

LOCATION	
⚡ ENERGY	☆☆☆☆☆
🏃 ACTIVITY	☆☆☆☆☆
🌙 SLEEP	☆☆☆☆☆

DAILY GOALS

- ☐
- ☐
- ☐

NEGATIVE EVENTS

SYMPTOMS	TRIGGERS

MOOD TRACKER

N/A (SLEEP)	JOY	NUMBNESS
SADNESS	FEAR	ANGER

NOTES

ANXIETY JOURNAL

LOCATION		DAILY GOALS

⚡ ENERGY	☆ ☆ ☆ ☆ ☆
🏃 ACTIVITY	☆ ☆ ☆ ☆ ☆
🌙 SLEEP	☆ ☆ ☆ ☆ ☆

DAILY GOALS
- [ ]
- [ ]
- [ ]

NEGATIVE EVENTS

SYMPTOMS	TRIGGERS

MOOD TRACKER

N/A (SLEEP)	JOY	NUMBNESS
SADNESS	FEAR	ANGER

NOTES

ANXIETY JOURNAL

⊙ LOCATION		
⚡ ENERGY	☆☆☆☆☆	
🏃 ACTIVITY	☆☆☆☆☆	
🌙 SLEEP	☆☆☆☆☆	

DAILY GOALS

- ☐
- ☐
- ☐

NEGATIVE EVENTS

SYMPTOMS	TRIGGERS

MOOD TRACKER

▢ N/A (SLEEP)	▢ JOY	▢ NUMBNESS
▢ SADNESS	▢ FEAR	▢ ANGER

NOTES

ANXIETY JOURNAL

◎ LOCATION	

⚡ ENERGY	☆ ☆ ☆ ☆ ☆
🏃 ACTIVITY	☆ ☆ ☆ ☆ ☆
🌙 SLEEP	☆ ☆ ☆ ☆ ☆

DAILY GOALS

- [ ]
- [ ]
- [ ]

NEGATIVE EVENTS

SYMPTOMS	TRIGGERS

MOOD TRACKER

N/A (SLEEP)	JOY	NUMBNESS
SADNESS	FEAR	ANGER

NOTES

ANXIETY JOURNAL

⊙ LOCATION	
⚡ ENERGY	☆☆☆☆☆
🏃 ACTIVITY	☆☆☆☆☆
🌙 SLEEP	☆☆☆☆☆

DAILY GOALS

- ☐
- ☐
- ☐

NEGATIVE EVENTS

SYMPTOMS	TRIGGERS

MOOD TRACKER

▽	N/A (SLEEP)	▽	JOY	▽	NUMBNESS
▽	SADNESS	▽	FEAR	▽	ANGER

NOTES

ANXIETY JOURNAL

◎ LOCATION		
⚡ ENERGY	☆ ☆ ☆ ☆ ☆	
🏃 ACTIVITY	☆ ☆ ☆ ☆ ☆	
🌙 SLEEP	☆ ☆ ☆ ☆ ☆	

DAILY GOALS

- ☐
- ☐
- ☐

NEGATIVE EVENTS

SYMPTOMS	TRIGGERS

MOOD TRACKER

N/A (SLEEP)	JOY	NUMBNESS
SADNESS	FEAR	ANGER

NOTES

ANXIETY JOURNAL

⊙ LOCATION		
⚡ ENERGY	☆☆☆☆☆	
🏃 ACTIVITY	☆☆☆☆☆	
🌙 SLEEP	☆☆☆☆☆	

DAILY GOALS

- ☐
- ☐
- ☐

NEGATIVE EVENTS

SYMPTOMS	TRIGGERS

MOOD TRACKER

N/A (SLEEP)	JOY	NUMBNESS
SADNESS	FEAR	ANGER

NOTES

ANXIETY JOURNAL

⊙ LOCATION		DAILY GOALS	
⚡ ENERGY	☆☆☆☆☆	☐	
🏃 ACTIVITY	☆☆☆☆☆	☐	
🌙 SLEEP	☆☆☆☆☆	☐	

NEGATIVE EVENTS

SYMPTOMS	TRIGGERS

MOOD TRACKER

▭ N/A (SLEEP)	▭ JOY	▭ NUMBNESS
▭ SADNESS	▭ FEAR	▭ ANGER

NOTES

ANXIETY JOURNAL

⊚ LOCATION	
⚡ ENERGY	☆ ☆ ☆ ☆ ☆
🏃 ACTIVITY	☆ ☆ ☆ ☆ ☆
🌙 SLEEP	☆ ☆ ☆ ☆ ☆

DAILY GOALS

- ☐
- ☐
- ☐

NEGATIVE EVENTS

SYMPTOMS	TRIGGERS

MOOD TRACKER

N/A (SLEEP)	JOY	NUMBNESS
SADNESS	FEAR	ANGER

NOTES	

ANXIETY JOURNAL

⊙ LOCATION		DAILY GOALS

⚡ ENERGY	☆ ☆ ☆ ☆ ☆
🏃 ACTIVITY	☆ ☆ ☆ ☆ ☆
🌙 SLEEP	☆ ☆ ☆ ☆ ☆

DAILY GOALS

- ☐
- ☐
- ☐

NEGATIVE EVENTS

SYMPTOMS	TRIGGERS

MOOD TRACKER

⬜ N/A (SLEEP)	⬜ JOY	⬜ NUMBNESS
⬜ SADNESS	⬜ FEAR	⬜ ANGER

NOTES	

ANXIETY JOURNAL

⊙ LOCATION	
⚡ ENERGY	☆ ☆ ☆ ☆ ☆
🏃 ACTIVITY	☆ ☆ ☆ ☆ ☆
🌙 SLEEP	☆ ☆ ☆ ☆ ☆

DAILY GOALS

- ☐
- ☐
- ☐

NEGATIVE EVENTS

SYMPTOMS	TRIGGERS

MOOD TRACKER

N/A (SLEEP)	JOY	NUMBNESS
SADNESS	FEAR	ANGER

NOTES	

ANXIETY JOURNAL

	LOCATION	
⚡	ENERGY	☆ ☆ ☆ ☆ ☆
🏃	ACTIVITY	☆ ☆ ☆ ☆ ☆
🌙	SLEEP	☆ ☆ ☆ ☆ ☆

DAILY GOALS

- [ ]
- [ ]
- [ ]

NEGATIVE EVENTS

SYMPTOMS	TRIGGERS

MOOD TRACKER

N/A (SLEEP)	JOY	NUMBNESS
SADNESS	FEAR	ANGER

NOTES

ANXIETY JOURNAL

Location		Daily Goals
⚡ ENERGY	☆ ☆ ☆ ☆ ☆	☐
🏃 ACTIVITY	☆ ☆ ☆ ☆ ☆	☐
🌙 SLEEP	☆ ☆ ☆ ☆ ☆	☐

NEGATIVE EVENTS

SYMPTOMS	TRIGGERS

MOOD TRACKER

N/A (SLEEP)	JOY	NUMBNESS
SADNESS	FEAR	ANGER

NOTES	

ANXIETY JOURNAL

⊙ LOCATION		DAILY GOALS	
⚡ ENERGY	☆ ☆ ☆ ☆ ☆	☐	
🏃 ACTIVITY	☆ ☆ ☆ ☆ ☆	☐	
☾ SLEEP	☆ ☆ ☆ ☆ ☆	☐	

NEGATIVE EVENTS

SYMPTOMS	TRIGGERS

MOOD TRACKER

▽	N/A (SLEEP)	▽	JOY	▽	NUMBNESS
▽	SADNESS	▽	FEAR	▽	ANGER

NOTES	

ANXIETY JOURNAL

⊙ LOCATION	
⚡ ENERGY	☆ ☆ ☆ ☆ ☆
🏃 ACTIVITY	☆ ☆ ☆ ☆ ☆
🌙 SLEEP	☆ ☆ ☆ ☆ ☆

DAILY GOALS

- ☐
- ☐
- ☐

NEGATIVE EVENTS

SYMPTOMS	TRIGGERS

MOOD TRACKER

N/A (SLEEP)	JOY	NUMBNESS
SADNESS	FEAR	ANGER

NOTES

ANXIETY JOURNAL

⊙ LOCATION		DAILY GOALS	
⚡ ENERGY	☆ ☆ ☆ ☆ ☆	☐	
🏃 ACTIVITY	☆ ☆ ☆ ☆ ☆	☐	
🌙 SLEEP	☆ ☆ ☆ ☆ ☆	☐	

NEGATIVE EVENTS

SYMPTOMS	TRIGGERS

MOOD TRACKER

N/A (SLEEP)	JOY	NUMBNESS
SADNESS	FEAR	ANGER

NOTES

ANXIETY JOURNAL

◎ LOCATION	
⚡ ENERGY	☆ ☆ ☆ ☆ ☆
🏃 ACTIVITY	☆ ☆ ☆ ☆ ☆
🌙 SLEEP	☆ ☆ ☆ ☆ ☆

DAILY GOALS

- [ ]
- [ ]
- [ ]

NEGATIVE EVENTS

SYMPTOMS	TRIGGERS

MOOD TRACKER

	N/A (SLEEP)		JOY		NUMBNESS
	SADNESS		FEAR		ANGER

NOTES

ANXIETY JOURNAL

⊙ LOCATION		DAILY GOALS	
⚡ ENERGY	☆ ☆ ☆ ☆ ☆	☐	
🏃 ACTIVITY	☆ ☆ ☆ ☆ ☆	☐	
🌙 SLEEP	☆ ☆ ☆ ☆ ☆	☐	

NEGATIVE EVENTS

SYMPTOMS	TRIGGERS

MOOD TRACKER

⊔	N/A (SLEEP)	⊔	JOY	⊔	NUMBNESS
⊔	SADNESS	⊔	FEAR	⊔	ANGER

NOTES

ANXIETY JOURNAL

⊙ LOCATION		DAILY GOALS	

⚡ ENERGY	☆ ☆ ☆ ☆ ☆	☐
🏃 ACTIVITY	☆ ☆ ☆ ☆ ☆	☐
🌙 SLEEP	☆ ☆ ☆ ☆ ☆	☐

NEGATIVE EVENTS

SYMPTOMS	TRIGGERS

MOOD TRACKER

N/A (SLEEP)	JOY	NUMBNESS
SADNESS	FEAR	ANGER

NOTES	

ANXIETY JOURNAL

LOCATION	
⚡ ENERGY	☆ ☆ ☆ ☆ ☆
🏃 ACTIVITY	☆ ☆ ☆ ☆ ☆
🌙 SLEEP	☆ ☆ ☆ ☆ ☆

DAILY GOALS

- [ ]
- [ ]
- [ ]

NEGATIVE EVENTS

SYMPTOMS	TRIGGERS

MOOD TRACKER

N/A (SLEEP)	JOY	NUMBNESS
SADNESS	FEAR	ANGER

NOTES

ANXIETY JOURNAL

⊙ LOCATION		DAILY GOALS

⚡ ENERGY	☆ ☆ ☆ ☆ ☆	☐
🏃 ACTIVITY	☆ ☆ ☆ ☆ ☆	☐
🌙 SLEEP	☆ ☆ ☆ ☆ ☆	☐

NEGATIVE EVENTS

SYMPTOMS	TRIGGERS

MOOD TRACKER

N/A (SLEEP)	JOY	NUMBNESS
SADNESS	FEAR	ANGER

NOTES	

ANXIETY JOURNAL

⊙ LOCATION	
⚡ ENERGY	☆ ☆ ☆ ☆ ☆
🏃 ACTIVITY	☆ ☆ ☆ ☆ ☆
🌙 SLEEP	☆ ☆ ☆ ☆ ☆

DAILY GOALS

- ☐
- ☐
- ☐

NEGATIVE EVENTS

SYMPTOMS	TRIGGERS

MOOD TRACKER

N/A (SLEEP)	JOY	NUMBNESS
SADNESS	FEAR	ANGER

NOTES

ANXIETY JOURNAL

⊙ LOCATION	
⚡ ENERGY	☆ ☆ ☆ ☆ ☆
🏃 ACTIVITY	☆ ☆ ☆ ☆ ☆
☾ SLEEP	☆ ☆ ☆ ☆ ☆

DAILY GOALS

- ☐
- ☐
- ☐

NEGATIVE EVENTS

SYMPTOMS	TRIGGERS

MOOD TRACKER

▭ N/A (SLEEP)	▭ JOY	▭ NUMBNESS
▭ SADNESS	▭ FEAR	▭ ANGER

NOTES

ANXIETY JOURNAL

⊙ LOCATION		
⚡ ENERGY	☆☆☆☆☆	
🏃 ACTIVITY	☆☆☆☆☆	
🌙 SLEEP	☆☆☆☆☆	

DAILY GOALS

- ☐
- ☐
- ☐

NEGATIVE EVENTS

SYMPTOMS	TRIGGERS

MOOD TRACKER

N/A (SLEEP)	JOY	NUMBNESS
SADNESS	FEAR	ANGER

NOTES

ANXIETY JOURNAL

⊚ LOCATION	
⚡ ENERGY	☆ ☆ ☆ ☆ ☆
🏃 ACTIVITY	☆ ☆ ☆ ☆ ☆
🌙 SLEEP	☆ ☆ ☆ ☆ ☆

DAILY GOALS

- ☐
- ☐
- ☐

NEGATIVE EVENTS

SYMPTOMS	TRIGGERS

MOOD TRACKER

▢ N/A (SLEEP)	▢ JOY	▢ NUMBNESS
▢ SADNESS	▢ FEAR	▢ ANGER

NOTES

ANXIETY JOURNAL

◎ LOCATION		DAILY GOALS	
⚡ ENERGY	☆ ☆ ☆ ☆ ☆	☐	
🏃 ACTIVITY	☆ ☆ ☆ ☆ ☆	☐	
🌙 SLEEP	☆ ☆ ☆ ☆ ☆	☐	

NEGATIVE EVENTS

SYMPTOMS	TRIGGERS

MOOD TRACKER

N/A (SLEEP)	JOY	NUMBNESS
SADNESS	FEAR	ANGER

NOTES

ANXIETY JOURNAL

◎ LOCATION	
⚡ ENERGY	☆☆☆☆☆
🏃 ACTIVITY	☆☆☆☆☆
🌙 SLEEP	☆☆☆☆☆

DAILY GOALS

- ☐
- ☐
- ☐

NEGATIVE EVENTS

SYMPTOMS	TRIGGERS

MOOD TRACKER

N/A (SLEEP)	JOY	NUMBNESS
SADNESS	FEAR	ANGER

NOTES

ANXIETY JOURNAL

⊙ LOCATION		DAILY GOALS

⚡ ENERGY	☆ ☆ ☆ ☆ ☆	☐
🏃 ACTIVITY	☆ ☆ ☆ ☆ ☆	☐
🌙 SLEEP	☆ ☆ ☆ ☆ ☆	☐

NEGATIVE EVENTS

SYMPTOMS	TRIGGERS

MOOD TRACKER

N/A (SLEEP)	JOY	NUMBNESS
SADNESS	FEAR	ANGER

NOTES

ANXIETY JOURNAL

LOCATION	
⚡ ENERGY	☆☆☆☆☆
🏃 ACTIVITY	☆☆☆☆☆
🌙 SLEEP	☆☆☆☆☆

DAILY GOALS

- ☐
- ☐
- ☐

NEGATIVE EVENTS

SYMPTOMS	TRIGGERS

MOOD TRACKER

N/A (SLEEP)	JOY	NUMBNESS
SADNESS	FEAR	ANGER

NOTES

ANXIETY JOURNAL

LOCATION		DAILY GOALS	

⚡ ENERGY	☆ ☆ ☆ ☆ ☆	☐
🏃 ACTIVITY	☆ ☆ ☆ ☆ ☆	☐
🌙 SLEEP	☆ ☆ ☆ ☆ ☆	☐

NEGATIVE EVENTS

SYMPTOMS	TRIGGERS

MOOD TRACKER

	N/A (SLEEP)		JOY		NUMBNESS
	SADNESS		FEAR		ANGER

NOTES

ANXIETY JOURNAL

⊙ LOCATION		DAILY GOALS	
⚡ ENERGY	☆☆☆☆☆	☐	
🏃 ACTIVITY	☆☆☆☆☆	☐	
🌙 SLEEP	☆☆☆☆☆	☐	

NEGATIVE EVENTS

SYMPTOMS	TRIGGERS

MOOD TRACKER

	N/A (SLEEP)		JOY		NUMBNESS
	SADNESS		FEAR		ANGER

NOTES

ANXIETY JOURNAL

⊙ LOCATION	
⚡ ENERGY	☆ ☆ ☆ ☆ ☆
🏃 ACTIVITY	☆ ☆ ☆ ☆ ☆
🌙 SLEEP	☆ ☆ ☆ ☆ ☆

DAILY GOALS

- ☐
- ☐
- ☐

NEGATIVE EVENTS

SYMPTOMS	TRIGGERS

MOOD TRACKER

	N/A (SLEEP)		JOY		NUMBNESS
	SADNESS		FEAR		ANGER

NOTES

ANXIETY JOURNAL

◎ LOCATION	
⚡ ENERGY	☆ ☆ ☆ ☆ ☆
🏃 ACTIVITY	☆ ☆ ☆ ☆ ☆
🌙 SLEEP	☆ ☆ ☆ ☆ ☆

DAILY GOALS

- ☐
- ☐
- ☐

NEGATIVE EVENTS

SYMPTOMS	TRIGGERS

MOOD TRACKER

▽ N/A (SLEEP)	▽ JOY	▽ NUMBNESS
▽ SADNESS	▽ FEAR	▽ ANGER

NOTES

ANXIETY JOURNAL

⚲ LOCATION					
⚡ ENERGY	☆	☆	☆	☆	☆
🏃 ACTIVITY	☆	☆	☆	☆	☆
🌙 SLEEP	☆	☆	☆	☆	☆

DAILY GOALS

- ☐
- ☐
- ☐

NEGATIVE EVENTS

SYMPTOMS	TRIGGERS

MOOD TRACKER

N/A (SLEEP)	JOY	NUMBNESS
SADNESS	FEAR	ANGER

NOTES

ANXIETY JOURNAL

⊙ LOCATION		DAILY GOALS	

⚡ ENERGY	☆ ☆ ☆ ☆ ☆
🏃 ACTIVITY	☆ ☆ ☆ ☆ ☆
🌙 SLEEP	☆ ☆ ☆ ☆ ☆

DAILY GOALS

- ☐
- ☐
- ☐

NEGATIVE EVENTS

SYMPTOMS	TRIGGERS

MOOD TRACKER

	N/A (SLEEP)		JOY		NUMBNESS
	SADNESS		FEAR		ANGER

NOTES

ANXIETY JOURNAL

⊙ LOCATION			
⚡ ENERGY	☆ ☆ ☆ ☆ ☆		
🏃 ACTIVITY	☆ ☆ ☆ ☆ ☆		
🌙 SLEEP	☆ ☆ ☆ ☆ ☆		

DAILY GOALS

- ☐
- ☐
- ☐

NEGATIVE EVENTS

SYMPTOMS	TRIGGERS

MOOD TRACKER

▢ N/A (SLEEP)		▢ JOY		▢ NUMBNESS	
▢ SADNESS		▢ FEAR		▢ ANGER	

NOTES

ANXIETY JOURNAL

LOCATION	
⚡ ENERGY	☆ ☆ ☆ ☆ ☆
🏃 ACTIVITY	☆ ☆ ☆ ☆ ☆
🌙 SLEEP	☆ ☆ ☆ ☆ ☆

DAILY GOALS

- ☐
- ☐
- ☐

NEGATIVE EVENTS

SYMPTOMS	TRIGGERS

MOOD TRACKER

N/A (SLEEP)	JOY	NUMBNESS
SADNESS	FEAR	ANGER

NOTES

ANXIETY JOURNAL

⊙ LOCATION		DAILY GOALS

⚡ ENERGY	☆ ☆ ☆ ☆ ☆
🏃 ACTIVITY	☆ ☆ ☆ ☆ ☆
🌙 SLEEP	☆ ☆ ☆ ☆ ☆

Daily Goals checkboxes:
- ☐
- ☐
- ☐

NEGATIVE EVENTS

SYMPTOMS	TRIGGERS

MOOD TRACKER

N/A (SLEEP)	JOY	NUMBNESS
SADNESS	FEAR	ANGER

NOTES

ANXIETY JOURNAL

◎ LOCATION	
⚡ ENERGY	☆ ☆ ☆ ☆ ☆
🏃 ACTIVITY	☆ ☆ ☆ ☆ ☆
🌙 SLEEP	☆ ☆ ☆ ☆ ☆

DAILY GOALS

☐

☐

☐

NEGATIVE EVENTS

SYMPTOMS	TRIGGERS

MOOD TRACKER

N/A (SLEEP)	JOY	NUMBNESS
SADNESS	FEAR	ANGER

NOTES

ANXIETY JOURNAL

⊙ LOCATION	
⚡ ENERGY ☆☆☆☆☆	
🏃 ACTIVITY ☆☆☆☆☆	
🌙 SLEEP ☆☆☆☆☆	

DAILY GOALS

- ☐
- ☐
- ☐

NEGATIVE EVENTS

SYMPTOMS	TRIGGERS

MOOD TRACKER

N/A (SLEEP)	JOY	NUMBNESS
SADNESS	FEAR	ANGER

NOTES

ANXIETY JOURNAL

LOCATION		DAILY GOALS

⚡ ENERGY	☆ ☆ ☆ ☆ ☆
🏃 ACTIVITY	☆ ☆ ☆ ☆ ☆
🌙 SLEEP	☆ ☆ ☆ ☆ ☆

DAILY GOALS

☐
☐
☐

NEGATIVE EVENTS

SYMPTOMS	TRIGGERS

MOOD TRACKER

	N/A (SLEEP)		JOY		NUMBNESS
	SADNESS		FEAR		ANGER

NOTES

ANXIETY JOURNAL

LOCATION						DAILY GOALS	

⚡ ENERGY	☆ ☆ ☆ ☆ ☆	☐
🏃 ACTIVITY	☆ ☆ ☆ ☆ ☆	☐
🌙 SLEEP	☆ ☆ ☆ ☆ ☆	☐

NEGATIVE EVENTS

SYMPTOMS	TRIGGERS

MOOD TRACKER

N/A (SLEEP)	JOY	NUMBNESS
SADNESS	FEAR	ANGER

NOTES

ANXIETY JOURNAL

◎ LOCATION	
⚡ ENERGY	☆ ☆ ☆ ☆ ☆
🏃 ACTIVITY	☆ ☆ ☆ ☆ ☆
🌙 SLEEP	☆ ☆ ☆ ☆ ☆

DAILY GOALS

- ☐
- ☐
- ☐

NEGATIVE EVENTS

SYMPTOMS	TRIGGERS

MOOD TRACKER

▢ N/A (SLEEP)	▢ JOY	▢ NUMBNESS
▢ SADNESS	▢ FEAR	▢ ANGER

NOTES	

ANXIETY JOURNAL

⊙ LOCATION	
⚡ ENERGY	☆ ☆ ☆ ☆ ☆
🏃 ACTIVITY	☆ ☆ ☆ ☆ ☆
🌙 SLEEP	☆ ☆ ☆ ☆ ☆

DAILY GOALS

☐

☐

☐

NEGATIVE EVENTS

SYMPTOMS	TRIGGERS

MOOD TRACKER

N/A (SLEEP)	JOY	NUMBNESS
SADNESS	FEAR	ANGER

NOTES

ANXIETY JOURNAL

◎ LOCATION	

⚡ ENERGY	☆ ☆ ☆ ☆ ☆
🏃 ACTIVITY	☆ ☆ ☆ ☆ ☆
🌙 SLEEP	☆ ☆ ☆ ☆ ☆

DAILY GOALS

- ☐
- ☐
- ☐

NEGATIVE EVENTS

SYMPTOMS	TRIGGERS

MOOD TRACKER

N/A (SLEEP)	JOY	NUMBNESS
SADNESS	FEAR	ANGER

NOTES

ANXIETY JOURNAL

⊙ LOCATION		DAILY GOALS

ϟ ENERGY	☆ ☆ ☆ ☆ ☆
🏃 ACTIVITY	☆ ☆ ☆ ☆ ☆
🌙 SLEEP	☆ ☆ ☆ ☆ ☆

DAILY GOALS
- ☐
- ☐
- ☐

NEGATIVE EVENTS

SYMPTOMS	TRIGGERS

MOOD TRACKER

⊔ N/A (SLEEP)	⊔ JOY	⊔ NUMBNESS
⊔ SADNESS	⊔ FEAR	⊔ ANGER

NOTES	

ANXIETY JOURNAL

⊙ LOCATION	
⚡ ENERGY	☆ ☆ ☆ ☆ ☆
🏃 ACTIVITY	☆ ☆ ☆ ☆ ☆
☾ SLEEP	☆ ☆ ☆ ☆ ☆

DAILY GOALS

- ☐
- ☐
- ☐

NEGATIVE EVENTS

SYMPTOMS	TRIGGERS

MOOD TRACKER

N/A (SLEEP)	JOY	NUMBNESS
SADNESS	FEAR	ANGER

NOTES	

ANXIETY JOURNAL

⊙ LOCATION		
⚡ ENERGY	☆ ☆ ☆ ☆ ☆	
🏃 ACTIVITY	☆ ☆ ☆ ☆ ☆	
🌙 SLEEP	☆ ☆ ☆ ☆ ☆	

DAILY GOALS

- ☐
- ☐
- ☐

NEGATIVE EVENTS

SYMPTOMS	TRIGGERS

MOOD TRACKER

N/A (SLEEP)	JOY	NUMBNESS
SADNESS	FEAR	ANGER

NOTES

ANXIETY JOURNAL

⊙ LOCATION		DAILY GOALS	
⚡ ENERGY	☆☆☆☆☆	☐	
🏃 ACTIVITY	☆☆☆☆☆	☐	
🌙 SLEEP	☆☆☆☆☆	☐	

NEGATIVE EVENTS

SYMPTOMS	TRIGGERS

MOOD TRACKER

N/A (SLEEP)		JOY		NUMBNESS	
SADNESS		FEAR		ANGER	

NOTES	

ANXIETY JOURNAL

⊙ LOCATION		DAILY GOALS

⚡ ENERGY	☆ ☆ ☆ ☆ ☆	☐
🏃 ACTIVITY	☆ ☆ ☆ ☆ ☆	☐
☾ SLEEP	☆ ☆ ☆ ☆ ☆	☐

NEGATIVE EVENTS

SYMPTOMS	TRIGGERS

MOOD TRACKER

▭ N/A (SLEEP)	▭ JOY	▭ NUMBNESS
▭ SADNESS	▭ FEAR	▭ ANGER

NOTES	

ANXIETY JOURNAL

⊙ LOCATION	
⚡ ENERGY	☆ ☆ ☆ ☆ ☆
🏃 ACTIVITY	☆ ☆ ☆ ☆ ☆
🌙 SLEEP	☆ ☆ ☆ ☆ ☆

DAILY GOALS

- ☐
- ☐
- ☐

NEGATIVE EVENTS

SYMPTOMS	TRIGGERS

MOOD TRACKER

☐	N/A (SLEEP)	☐	JOY	☐	NUMBNESS
☐	SADNESS	☐	FEAR	☐	ANGER

NOTES

ANXIETY JOURNAL

◎ LOCATION		DAILY GOALS	
⚡ ENERGY	☆ ☆ ☆ ☆ ☆	☐	
🏃 ACTIVITY	☆ ☆ ☆ ☆ ☆	☐	
🌙 SLEEP	☆ ☆ ☆ ☆ ☆	☐	

NEGATIVE EVENTS

SYMPTOMS	TRIGGERS

MOOD TRACKER

N/A (SLEEP)	JOY	NUMBNESS
SADNESS	FEAR	ANGER

NOTES

ANXIETY JOURNAL

⊚ LOCATION	
⚡ ENERGY	☆☆☆☆☆
🏃 ACTIVITY	☆☆☆☆☆
🌙 SLEEP	☆☆☆☆☆

DAILY GOALS

- ☐
- ☐
- ☐

NEGATIVE EVENTS

SYMPTOMS	TRIGGERS

MOOD TRACKER

	N/A (SLEEP)		JOY		NUMBNESS
	SADNESS		FEAR		ANGER

NOTES	

ANXIETY JOURNAL

⊚ LOCATION		
⚡ ENERGY	☆ ☆ ☆ ☆ ☆	
🏃 ACTIVITY	☆ ☆ ☆ ☆ ☆	
🌙 SLEEP	☆ ☆ ☆ ☆ ☆	

DAILY GOALS

- ☐
- ☐
- ☐

NEGATIVE EVENTS

SYMPTOMS	TRIGGERS

MOOD TRACKER

☐ N/A (SLEEP)	☐ JOY	☐ NUMBNESS
☐ SADNESS	☐ FEAR	☐ ANGER

NOTES

ANXIETY JOURNAL

⊙ LOCATION		DAILY GOALS	

⚡ ENERGY	☆ ☆ ☆ ☆ ☆
🏃 ACTIVITY	☆ ☆ ☆ ☆ ☆
🌙 SLEEP	☆ ☆ ☆ ☆ ☆

DAILY GOALS
- ☐
- ☐
- ☐

NEGATIVE EVENTS

SYMPTOMS	TRIGGERS

MOOD TRACKER

	N/A (SLEEP)		JOY		NUMBNESS
	SADNESS		FEAR		ANGER

NOTES	

ANXIETY JOURNAL

⊙ LOCATION		DAILY GOALS

⚡ ENERGY	☆ ☆ ☆ ☆ ☆	☐
🏃 ACTIVITY	☆ ☆ ☆ ☆ ☆	☐
🌙 SLEEP	☆ ☆ ☆ ☆ ☆	☐

NEGATIVE EVENTS

SYMPTOMS	TRIGGERS

MOOD TRACKER

▢ N/A (SLEEP)	▢ JOY	▢ NUMBNESS
▢ SADNESS	▢ FEAR	▢ ANGER

NOTES	

ANXIETY JOURNAL

	LOCATION		DAILY GOALS	

☇ ENERGY ☆☆☆☆☆

🏃 ACTIVITY ☆☆☆☆☆

☾ SLEEP ☆☆☆☆☆

DAILY GOALS

☐

☐

☐

NEGATIVE EVENTS

SYMPTOMS	TRIGGERS

MOOD TRACKER

	N/A (SLEEP)		JOY		NUMBNESS
	SADNESS		FEAR		ANGER

NOTES

ANXIETY JOURNAL

LOCATION		DAILY GOALS	
⚡ ENERGY	☆ ☆ ☆ ☆ ☆	☐	
🏃 ACTIVITY	☆ ☆ ☆ ☆ ☆	☐	
🌙 SLEEP	☆ ☆ ☆ ☆ ☆	☐	

NEGATIVE EVENTS

SYMPTOMS	TRIGGERS

MOOD TRACKER

N/A (SLEEP)	JOY	NUMBNESS
SADNESS	FEAR	ANGER

NOTES

ANXIETY JOURNAL

⊙ LOCATION	
⚡ ENERGY	☆ ☆ ☆ ☆ ☆
🏃 ACTIVITY	☆ ☆ ☆ ☆ ☆
🌙 SLEEP	☆ ☆ ☆ ☆ ☆

DAILY GOALS

☐
☐
☐

NEGATIVE EVENTS

SYMPTOMS	TRIGGERS

MOOD TRACKER

▽ N/A (SLEEP)	▽ JOY	▽ NUMBNESS
▽ SADNESS	▽ FEAR	▽ ANGER

NOTES

ANXIETY JOURNAL

⊙ LOCATION	
⚡ ENERGY	☆ ☆ ☆ ☆ ☆
🏃 ACTIVITY	☆ ☆ ☆ ☆ ☆
☾ SLEEP	☆ ☆ ☆ ☆ ☆

DAILY GOALS

- ☐
- ☐
- ☐

NEGATIVE EVENTS

SYMPTOMS	TRIGGERS

MOOD TRACKER

N/A (SLEEP)	JOY	NUMBNESS
SADNESS	FEAR	ANGER

NOTES

ANXIETY JOURNAL

LOCATION	
⚡ ENERGY	☆☆☆☆☆
🏃 ACTIVITY	☆☆☆☆☆
🌙 SLEEP	☆☆☆☆☆

DAILY GOALS

- ☐
- ☐
- ☐

NEGATIVE EVENTS

SYMPTOMS	TRIGGERS

MOOD TRACKER

N/A (SLEEP)	JOY	NUMBNESS
SADNESS	FEAR	ANGER

NOTES

ANXIETY JOURNAL

⊙ LOCATION		DAILY GOALS

⚡ ENERGY	☆ ☆ ☆ ☆ ☆	☐
🏃 ACTIVITY	☆ ☆ ☆ ☆ ☆	☐
🌙 SLEEP	☆ ☆ ☆ ☆ ☆	☐

NEGATIVE EVENTS

SYMPTOMS	TRIGGERS

MOOD TRACKER

	N/A (SLEEP)		JOY		NUMBNESS
	SADNESS		FEAR		ANGER

NOTES	

ANXIETY JOURNAL

⊙ LOCATION		DAILY GOALS	
⚡ ENERGY	☆ ☆ ☆ ☆ ☆	☐	
🏃 ACTIVITY	☆ ☆ ☆ ☆ ☆	☐	
🌙 SLEEP	☆ ☆ ☆ ☆ ☆	☐	

NEGATIVE EVENTS

SYMPTOMS	TRIGGERS

MOOD TRACKER

	N/A (SLEEP)		JOY		NUMBNESS
	SADNESS		FEAR		ANGER

NOTES

ANXIETY JOURNAL

⊙ LOCATION		DAILY GOALS	

⚡ ENERGY	☆ ☆ ☆ ☆ ☆	☐
🏃 ACTIVITY	☆ ☆ ☆ ☆ ☆	☐
🌙 SLEEP	☆ ☆ ☆ ☆ ☆	☐

NEGATIVE EVENTS

SYMPTOMS	TRIGGERS

MOOD TRACKER

▽ N/A (SLEEP)	▽ JOY	▽ NUMBNESS
▽ SADNESS	▽ FEAR	▽ ANGER

NOTES	

ANXIETY JOURNAL

◎ LOCATION	
⚡ ENERGY	☆ ☆ ☆ ☆ ☆
🏃 ACTIVITY	☆ ☆ ☆ ☆ ☆
🌙 SLEEP	☆ ☆ ☆ ☆ ☆

DAILY GOALS

- ☐
- ☐
- ☐

NEGATIVE EVENTS

SYMPTOMS	TRIGGERS

MOOD TRACKER

N/A (SLEEP)	JOY	NUMBNESS
SADNESS	FEAR	ANGER

NOTES

ANXIETY JOURNAL

LOCATION		DAILY GOALS	
⚡ ENERGY	☆ ☆ ☆ ☆ ☆	☐	
🏃 ACTIVITY	☆ ☆ ☆ ☆ ☆	☐	
🌙 SLEEP	☆ ☆ ☆ ☆ ☆	☐	

NEGATIVE EVENTS

SYMPTOMS	TRIGGERS

MOOD TRACKER

	N/A (SLEEP)		JOY		NUMBNESS
	SADNESS		FEAR		ANGER

NOTES

ANXIETY JOURNAL

⊙ LOCATION	
⚡ ENERGY	☆ ☆ ☆ ☆ ☆
🏃 ACTIVITY	☆ ☆ ☆ ☆ ☆
🌙 SLEEP	☆ ☆ ☆ ☆ ☆

DAILY GOALS

- ☐
- ☐
- ☐

NEGATIVE EVENTS

SYMPTOMS	TRIGGERS

MOOD TRACKER

N/A (SLEEP)	JOY	NUMBNESS
SADNESS	FEAR	ANGER

NOTES	

ANXIETY JOURNAL

		DAILY GOALS
⊙ LOCATION		
⚡ ENERGY	☆ ☆ ☆ ☆ ☆	☐
🏃 ACTIVITY	☆ ☆ ☆ ☆ ☆	☐
☾ SLEEP	☆ ☆ ☆ ☆ ☆	☐

NEGATIVE EVENTS

SYMPTOMS	TRIGGERS

MOOD TRACKER

▽ N/A (SLEEP)	▽ JOY	▽ NUMBNESS
▽ SADNESS	▽ FEAR	▽ ANGER

NOTES

ANXIETY JOURNAL

⊙ LOCATION	
⚡ ENERGY	☆☆☆☆☆
🏃 ACTIVITY	☆☆☆☆☆
🌙 SLEEP	☆☆☆☆☆

DAILY GOALS

- [ ]
- [ ]
- [ ]

NEGATIVE EVENTS

SYMPTOMS	TRIGGERS

MOOD TRACKER

N/A (SLEEP)	JOY	NUMBNESS
SADNESS	FEAR	ANGER

NOTES

ANXIETY JOURNAL

⊙ LOCATION		
⚡ ENERGY	☆ ☆ ☆ ☆ ☆	
🏃 ACTIVITY	☆ ☆ ☆ ☆ ☆	
🌙 SLEEP	☆ ☆ ☆ ☆ ☆	

DAILY GOALS

- ☐
- ☐
- ☐

NEGATIVE EVENTS

SYMPTOMS	TRIGGERS

MOOD TRACKER

▽ N/A (SLEEP)	▽ JOY	▽ NUMBNESS
▽ SADNESS	▽ FEAR	▽ ANGER

NOTES

Made in the USA
Las Vegas, NV
27 September 2022

56025575R00070